Blockchain:

Beginner's Guide To Explore
The Technology, Cryptocurrency
Wallets, Mining And Other
Digital Coins

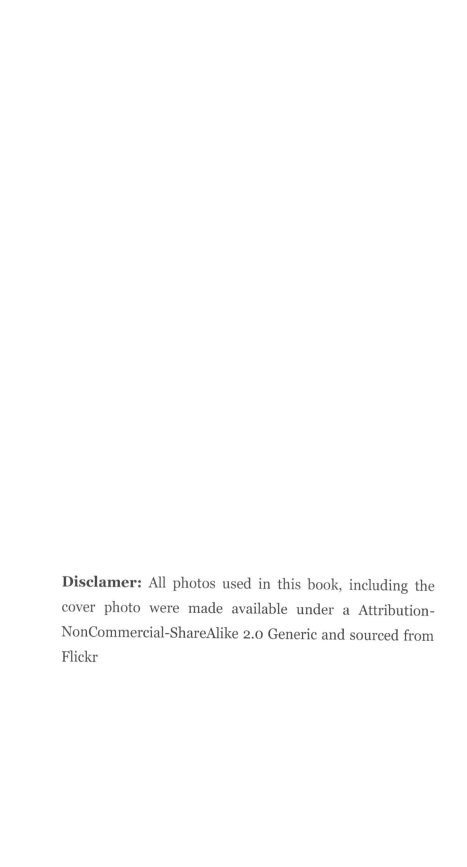

Table of Content:

Introduction

Nowadays cryptocurrencies have become a part and parcel of our lives. Perhaps, only the hermit who has refused all the benefits of civilization does not know about the famous Bitcoin. But when people use this concept in their everyday speech, they tend to operate such word as bitchain.

For an inexperienced in finances personality, blockchain may seem like a specific tool that works only in Bitcoin, but in fact this is the technology which supports the vast majority of all cryptocurrencies internationally. If you want to understand cryptocurrencies and get familiar with their specifics, you should definitely start with what blockchain is and how it functions.

After all, it is impossible to understand the essence of the entire system without firstly perceiving the basic principles of its operation. As we aim at people who have just started their travel in this wonderful world of cryptocurrency, don't expect for the complicated terms here. We will try to make the narration as easy as possible so than even a pupil could understand what we are talking about.

A great deal of business analysts calls this technology the biggest technical breakthrough since global society knew about the invention of the Internet. Although some people remain skeptical, it is already getting clear that progress cannot be stopped, and blockchain technology will have changed our life in a huge variety of ways.

Typically, the word blockchain itself reflects the essence of technology. The blockchain network is a kind of repository of digital information, where all data is recorded sequentially in the form of blocks. You can imagine it as a diary, the owner of which clearly records all his actions one by one, or an archive where data cards are added sequentially, and the next card will not be inserted until the previous one has taken place.

Blockchain technology is well-known for a high degree of decentralization and a level of security. The system does not possess a single centralized governing body; instead, the validity of transactions and transactions is confirmed by the system using computers of all network participants

That is, at the time of the transaction or transaction, an appropriate data is sent to all computers connected to the blockchain network, and when each of the computers provides confirmation, the transaction is considered completed. After that, transaction data is recorded in a block being separately stored on each computer in the network.

Such a system makes it possible to get rid of intermediaries, because, in fact, it acts as an assurance body for itself. As a result, work and exchange between clients is very accelerated. In addition, this approach provides the highest level of security.

After all, it is impossible to steal or replace information in one block without changing others. To do it, enormous computing power and a lot of time are needed. If you take into account that you need to hack more than one computer, but everything at once will reveal the substitution so quickly, the idea seems even theoretically unrealizable.

Chapter 1 – What is blockchain

The world learned in 2009 what the blockchain is after the launch of the famous cryptocurrency Bitcoin. However, the theoretical foundations for various implementations of this technology trace back to the nineties of the last century. The name of inventor has to be known for everybody as we talk about Adam Buck, Hal Finney, as well as Wei Dai and Nick Szabo.

It is believed that on the basis of these studies Japanese programmer Satoshi Nakamoto developed his blockchain technology. The processing began in 2007, according to a popular rumor in the network, after Satoshi angered high commissions for money transfers and other transactions in conventional payment systems.

Nakamoto decided to implement a system devoid of these shortcomings, and already in 2008 the first protocol was published on the network with the principles of a new type of electronic money - Bitcoin cryptocurrency. In around a year, after minor modifications, Satoshi transferred the client program to the public and created the first block in the Bitcoin system.

In the modern world, carrying out almost all financial transactions, we have to encounter intermediaries. In case of money transfer, banks serve as such intermediaries, and notaries act as the conclusion of transactions.

Of course, with each such transaction, intermediaries take a commission, due to which they earn. Using blockchain technology, we get rid of the need for intermediaries, since the system is built on the principles of self-testing and guarantees the honesty of the transaction.

Accordingly, now we do not need to pay a commission to third parties, and the transaction automatically becomes more profitable. In addition, the absence of extra links in the chain gives short transactions, or in other words, transactions become very fast, in some cases even instant.

At first, the banking sector tried, as far as possible, to deal with the new system, since it threatened to take away a significant part of their profits. However, it has now become clear that this prospect is far from the near future, and banks will exist with the blockchain for at least another ten years, and most likely, much longer.

As you know, it's pointless to fight progress, and if you can't overcome it, then use it. Now banks are actively introducing blockchain technology for interbank transfers, thereby saving very significant financial resources, and in the future this system may completely replace the already outdated SWIFT system.

Also, this technology is actively used by large corporations for transnational transactions. If earlier such deals were signed for weeks, now the process takes only a few days, and on such a scale, savings can amount to millions of dollars. The usage of this technology is not limited only to the financial sector.

In the future, this technology can tightly enter many areas of human activity. We want to introduce you to the four most likely ways to use blockchain in the near future:

First of all, this is the storage of digital certificates. As it has been found out, access to anonymous blockchain data without a key is almost impossible, which means that this system is very well suited for storing certificates.

Then, we should talk about the network administration. Since the system is perfectly protected from hacker attacks and internal errors, it is great for storing passwords and user lists.

Next, it comes down to the roof of ownership. With the help of blockchain technology, confirmation of property rights will become simple and convenient. To do this, the user will only need to enter information into their personal blockchain block.

Finally, we have to take into consideration the confirmation of access rights. Blockchain is very convenient for identification in the system, since this method has undeniable advantages over existing systems and at the same time will be cheaper.

Chapter 2 – How does blockchain work

In order to understand how the blockchain works better, we need to talk a little about such a concept as "mining". We have already known that blockchain is a kind of data warehouse that is constantly updated with new information about transactions.

However, since the system is decentralized, it cannot service itself, for this it needs participants who will provide their computers to store the body of the blockchain, as well as to calculate and confirm the transactions in exchange for a reward. In the world of cryptocurrencies, such people have been called miners, since the process of finding the right block of transactions is a bit like excavating in a mine in order to find valuable resources.

What is spread database

The process of forming a new blockchain block is based on the principles of cryptography using hashing algorithms. This is necessary in order to encrypt information about transactions and fit all the data about them into one line of code.

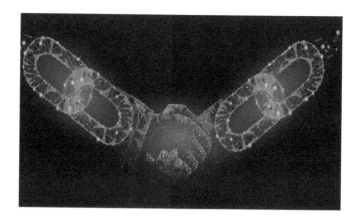

In fact, the block includes information about all transactions for a certain period of time, information about the previous block or its key, as well as random numbers to provide additional security. After that, a hash function is applied to the block to obtain a certain hash amount, which then becomes a unique signature of this block.

If all conditions have been met, the miner adds this block to the end of the blockchain, and information about this is copied to computers to all participants through a peer-to-peer network.

We have already touched on some of the advantages of the system a little higher, but a decentralized structure and high security is not all that the blockchain can boast of.

Thanks to the principles of cryptography, the system can be made open, but at the same time very anonymous. When a client completes a transaction within the system, he receives a unique key that is available only to him and his subscriber. Any user can view the archive of transactions and understand the dynamics of the development of the system, for example, one hundred dollars was sent to someone yesterday, but only key owners can see from whom and to whom.

Only with a key you can get unlimited access to information, which means that users are protected from the unfair use of personal data. In the modern world, when confidential information of private individuals merges into the network every day, this looks very relevant.

The difference between a traditional database and a blockchain begins with architecture, that shows how the technologies are organized. The familiar and long-known database most often uses the client-server network architecture. A user with permissions associated with his account can manage data stored on a central server, particularly, add, delete, and change them.

The management of the server part is left to the administrators. Indeed, they are engaged in technical support and restructuring, if necessary. They can also have different access levels that allow you to perform any action.

Blockchain can also be called a database, but its differences from classical databases are cardinal. On the blockchain, each participant maintains, calculates and updates records in the database. All nodes work together, all come to consensus, providing built-in network protection.

Due to its differences, each of the tools is suitable for different areas and tasks. The blockchain allows two parties that do not trust each other to exchange information without requiring an intermediary or central administrator. Transactions are processed by a network of users acting as a consensus mechanism that might be called as a mechanism of general agreement.

The importance of decentralized control is that it eliminates the risks of centralization. In the case of a single center, anyone with sufficient access to the system can destroy or corrupt data.

It makes users dependent on administrators. Banks are forced to spend billions so that their centralized bases are protected from losses. Most centralized databases contain information that is current at a specific time. They look like a picture that captured one moment.

A method that makes it possible for you to get previous snapshots is to create a backup. This procedure is performed regularly to restore data. The disadvantages of this approach are that each time you make a full copy of your database, and it can be quite large.

Databases on the blockchain can store information that is relevant now, as well as all the information that was before. Technology can create databases that have a history of themselves. This allows you to track any point in time.

Although blockchains can be used for writing and are ideal transaction platforms, they are considered slow compared to traditional options such as Visa and PayPal. Despite the fact that productivity will be improved in the future, the very nature of blockchain technology requires sacrificing speed to one degree or another.

The way the network is distributed on the blockchain means that the computing power is not shared or combined, each node independently maintains the network, and then compares the results of its work with the rest of the network until agreement is reached (consensus) that something happened.

Centralized databases, on the other hand, have been around for decades. They markedly increased their productivity with the help of a formula that began to determine innovation in the digital age. Particularly, it is Moore's law according to which the speed grows, limited only by the size of the atom and the speed of light.

Bitcoin is an uncontrolled record, an uncontrolled database. It means that theoretically anyone can write a new block in a chain and everybody is likely to read a block in a chain.

Despite the fact that the network or protocol can be configured so that only registered participants could write information or read it from the database (the rights system here may be similar to the classical one, or it may be a solution on the blockchain).

Hiding information in the blockchain requires deep cryptography and the associated computing load for network nodes. But this is still more efficient than a private database built on the classical system of rights.

We can conclude that if confidentiality is the only goal, and trust between the parties is established and there is no problem with storing large amounts of data (database backups), a database on the blockchain will not have any special advantages for you.

Blockchain is in demand, and 80% of the bases that are currently in use need the benefits it brings. This is the fuel that allows it to spread so quickly and receive great support. But there are also projects that do not impose such strict requirements on security, integrity, and distribution, so they can exist for many years without fundamentally changing their organization.

Types of blockchain

There are three different types of blockchain. This technology is constantly evolving and there may be more in the future.

Types of Blockchains

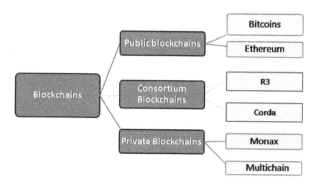

First of all, this is open blockchain, the most common and well-known type of this kind. Top cryptocurrencies like Bitcoin and Ethereum work based on it. Such a blockchain does not have a central authority confirming the operation. For example, let's pay attention towards Bitcoin blockchain that is a registry.

If I send somewhere a couple of coins, it will become known to the entire network and, if desired, any user will be able to verify the data of this transaction. This is how principle of public announcement works. The certain participants in the Bitcoin network receive a message about my transaction, and here the process of confirming the operation begins.

Also, it is impossible to find out in advance who will confirm the transaction. No user has privileges over confirmations. This is a very democratic system that allows any user to create smart contracts, send money or deposit data. Moreover, the type of network gives some anonymity.

Next, chain with different permission levels involve specific people who coordinate operations. It can be a central authority, an employee, an entire state or organization. Users can see the data, but important information can be hidden from them. Ordinary users cannot make entries; they can only view them. Blockchain is used for convenient interaction with customers of organizations working with different suppliers and goods. As in any other blockchain, all data remains on the network forever.

Well, there is something to be said about the closed block chain.This type is similar to an open blockchain with the exception of one detail; particularly, access to data viewing is issued privately.

This blockchain is used within two or more organizations. Operations between users are private information and can only be viewed by network participants. Data in the chain is recorded forever and read instantly.

Now you know more about the types of blockchain. Choosing the right registry type saves time and money. Since this industry began to develop not so long ago, in the future we will see even more innovation.

All types of blockchain are only conditional. Essentially, the technology remains the same - only some characteristics change. But specialists in the field of cryptocurrencies and blockchains have their own classifications of this system.

The founder of the Ethereum network, distinguishes 3 classes of blockchains:

- Public blockchain. It is completely open to participants and each of them can both carry out operations in it and participate in their administration.

- Blockchain owned by the consortium. In such blockchains, the matching procedure is assigned to pre-selected nodes.

- Private business center. Administration and coordination of procedures in such a network is carried out by a single body.

A similar classification is followed by the British government, Sir Mark Walport. He also identifies 3 types of blockchains, but calls them as open public registries, closed public registries, and private private registries.

Where to introduce blockchain technologies

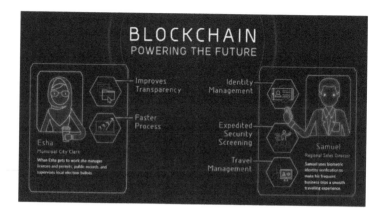

Along with banks and financial technical startups, players from other markets not related to the financial industry have also paid attention to technology. They are looking for ways to take advantage of the opportunities that it provides. Let's look at some interesting examples of practical applications of blockchain technology that exist outside the scope of financial services.

Ascribe helps artists and performers confirm and preserve copyright through the Blockchain. The Ascribe Marketplace allows you to create digital editions using unique identifiers and digital certificates to confirm authorship and authenticity.

In addition, a mechanism has been established to move ownership from the artist to the buyer, including its legal aspects. Other examples of services in this area are represented by Bitproof, Blockai, Stampery, Verisart, Monegraph, Crypto-Copyrightcrypto-copyright.com, Proof of Existence.

The Real Asset Company allows individuals in different countries to safely and efficiently buy gold and silver bullion. The company has developed an investor-friendly platform based on the international infrastructure of safes and vaults and providing customers with gold, silver or other precious metals an online account.

Goldbloc's gold-backed internal cryptocurrency adds an extra layer of transparency to the management of gold and foreign currency investments. According to the company, the capacity to "attach" gold to a digital cryptocurrency is likely to assist in returning it back to the financial systems of countries.

Uphold is a platform for moving, converting, making transactions and storing any form of money, goods or raw materials.

The service integrates banking operations, credit, debit cards and bitcoin wallets in the internal digital wallet of the service to simplify financial services or transactions. Businesses and individuals can transfer funds to their account in the system using bank transfer, debit, credit card, or bitcoin wallets.

Factom is a notable blockchain company that uses distributed registries outside the banking and money industry, in this case, in the area of informational security and management. The company's identification blockchains are used to implement a database management system and data analysis in various fields. Businesses and governments, non-for-profits use

Factom to simplify the procedures for maintaining records, recording data on various working processes. Factom solutions enable customers to conduct their business in compliance with the safety and demands of their market.

All entries in Factom have timestamps and are stored in blockchains, which reduces the cost and complexity of managing them, auditing, and compliance with regulatory requirements.

The diamond industry is one of the largest sectors of natural production, which also makes a significant contribution to the GDP of African and other diamond-mining countries. Its distinguishing feature is a high level of crime and violations of the law. Gemstones are very small in size and therefore easily amenable to hidden transport.

The most pleasant part for criminals is that transactions are carried out confidentially, and each sale at the same time allows you to make a profit for several years. Diamonds are notorious for money laundering tools and terrorist financing tools on a truly massive scale around the world.

One of the technology pioneering companies in this field, Everledger, is working to solve a number of such acute and difficult problems. It provides various interested parties from insurance companies and claimants with rights to law enforcement authorities with access to a register with unchanged historical data that allows you to identify diamonds and confirm the authenticity of transactions with them. The service issues a "digital passport" for each diamond - a kind of unique label that accompanies its gemstone in all its related transactions.

2WAY.IO, ShoCard, Guardtime, BlockVerify, HYPR, Onename and several other enterprises prefer distributed registry technology to work with the rights of access. The combination of the decentralized principle of blockchain and identity verification tools allows you to create a digital ID that plays the role of a kind of watermark that can be put on any transaction with any asset. Some other examples of companies in this area:

Civic is a blockchain-based identity management platform whose services are aimed at solving the problem of identity theft of customers. The service allows users to register, confirm personal information and protect their credit history from scammers.

UniquID Wallet provides a secure identity management solution that integrates with fingerprint scanners and other biometric personal devices. Work with the UniquID Wallet app is available on non-standard devices, servers, personal computers or smartphones, tablets and other devices with limited battery life. Among the declared capabilities, one can single out an individual blockchain storage for information about the used "devices" and the lack of passwords replaced by user recognition algorithms for personal objects connected to the system.

This allows you to achieve the highest possible level of integrity and interoperability within any infrastructure. Identifi connects all personal network profiles and personal data into a single identification tool.

Evernym is an international identity network created on the basis of its own high-speed, advanced distributed registry with separation of rights, designed to provide tools for controlling personal data. The source code of the project is open.

The founders of Energy Blockchain Labs claim that the company is the only company in the world whose activities are entirely devoted to the full cycle of creating added value in the energy industry.

Being founded in 2016 by three experienced specialists in the field of energy, finance and information technology, the laboratory is working on revolutionary solutions, including joint projects with other companies aimed at developing a number of Internet-based energy technologies based on Blockchain and solving problems in the field of development and energy consumption, trade, management and others.

There are other areas in the energy sector where talented entrepreneurs have managed to find a way to use decentralized distributed registries. Here are some interesting examples.

Grid Singularity is an industry-decentralized information exchange platform that provides a number of applications that simplify data analysis and testing, manage smart grids, work with green certificates and more.

LO3 Energy's TransActive Grid project is a cryptographically secure decentralized open source platform for applications. Built-in business logic tools allow you to measure the level of generation and consumption of electricity in real time, as well as some other indicators. The project is under development and the first demonstration installation is currently operating in the Brooklyn area of New York.

Follow My Vote is developing a secure and transparent platform for anonymous online voting using Blockchain technology and elliptical cryptography to guarantee the accuracy and reliability of the results. The source code of the project is open.

In February 2016, Nasdaq and the Estonian government announced that the state-owned e-Residency digital residency platform will be used to simplify the blockchain voting process at meetings of shareholders of companies listed on the country's only regulated Nasdaq's Tallinn Stock Exchange.

The e-Residency platform is an electronic identification system widely used both by Estonian residents and people who have business interests in the country and allowing all holders of relevant identification cards and digital keys to access a wide range of government, banking and other services.

Blockchain found its fans even in the gambling and video game industries - another striking example of the boundless and imaginative entrepreneurs.

Etheria is a virtual world where players try to take control of the cells of the playing field, mining them for blocks, and build something on them. All data describing the world and its state, as well as all actions of players are stored in a decentralized Ethereum blockchain

First Blood is a platform that allows cybersportsmen to challenge each other in different gaming disciplines, fans to place bets or judge games, as well as organize tournaments and receive rewards from any such activity. First Blood operates on the basis of the Ethereum blockchain with its own 1ST token, actively using smart contracts to process results and oracles as a source of information about the results of matches.

Etheramid is a cryptocurrency pyramid that calls itself the most honest invitational game ever created. The service charges ether's for each member for each invited new member (a total of 7 levels). The accrual algorithm is based on a self-governing smart contract, which neither the developers nor the owner of the pyramid are able to change.

The FreeMyVunk movement aims to enable the exchange of virtual property in video games. The platform exists in the form of a blockchain based on Ethereum, whose tokens (VUNK) act as an exchange currency. The authors of the idea offer all gamers of the world to join forces, join the network and earn VUNK, including through tweets and referral invitations

As for the gambling market, here, among others, you can bring such names as CoinPalace, Etheroll, Rollin, Ethereum Jackpot.

Blockchain can be applied not only to increase the transparency and integrity of political systems. In particular, there is a whole international virtual nation called BITNATION. She has her own citizens, ambassadors, partners and physical places around the world. Everyone can join it without any restrictions.

Another interesting example is Advocate, a platform for improving the interaction of citizens with government representatives, aimed at helping both ordinary members of the society and applicants for positions of managers in local government bodies.

It is also worth mentioning the Borderless management organization company - a civil management platform that positions itself as a coalition of legal (marriage, registration of legal entities, notary publicly accessible to the world) and economic services (basic income, financial transactions) based on smart contracts and the Expanse blockchain.

As for solutions for effective management within organizations, services such as Otonomos, BoardRoom and Colony exist for this purpose. Otonomos and BoardRoom automate the process of forming, financing and managing a company using Blockchain. Colony allows residents from around the world to create online companies.

Chronicled is a San Francisco-based company that launched a promising blockchain platform for the Internet of Things in August, aimed at improving the consumer experience.

As part of the project, the Ethereum blockchain stores the identification data of physical items, such as consumer goods and collectibles with built-in BLE and NFC microchips

This allows you to create safe and compatible with many other systems digital identifiers, which opens up opportunities for new mechanisms for interacting with the consumer, based on tracking his proximity to the subject. The Chronicled project is licensed under the Apache license, which is fully open source.

Filament offers a range of proprietary software and hardware solutions for large-scale smart control of industrial systems and equipment. The company's development is based on the principles of decentralization, cryptographic protection and autonomy.

Chimera service offers its own system of care for the elderly and people in need of care, as well as physical devices (bracelets, medallions) and applications for the remote collection and analysis of vital signs and determine situations when the person wearing them needs help.

Chapter 3 – Blockchain's advantages and disadvantages

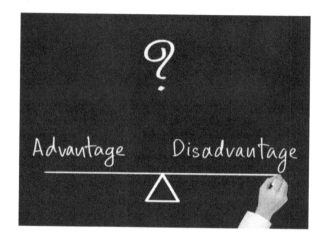

According to experts, today blockchain technology is a tool that has no equal in terms of protection, nor in simplicity and efficiency. Compared with other technologies for making electronic payments and storing confidential information, the blockchain has advantages and disadvantages.

Blockchain Benefits are the following ones:

- Storage at all members of the system at the same time, making it impossible to hack and steal;

- Transparency of transaction data. Thanks to this, any user can track information about the transfer of funds and make sure that the payment in the system was indeed sent;

- Irrevocability of all transactions. The payer cannot withdraw or freeze the sent money transfer "retroactively", thus deceiving the recipient;

- Transfer of codes of monetary units and other virtual values from the payer to the recipient directly, without the participation of intermediaries and without paying a commission.

It is the advantages of the blockchain that explain why this technology is called the "Internet of values". Using it, any network user can directly send money or intellectual values to a recipient from another country and even from another continent.

However, he can be sure that the transfer will not be stolen by attackers. The recipient, in turn, will be able to track the transaction and will know that the transfer will not be guaranteed to be recalled.

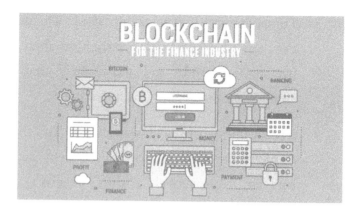

Creating Blockchain, Satoshi Nakamoto sought to create a system of payments on the network that would solve the question of trust between the payer and the recipient who are unfamiliar with each other. And he did it, because the principle of the technology allows you to make all transactions in the system secure, transparent and irrevocable.

This feature is definitely one of the main advantages of the blockchain. It means that blockchain technology in simple words is an instrument for transferring virtual values that has no analogues in transparency and security, which does not guarantee that the advantages and disadvantages of the blockchain will be in such a ratio that the latter cannot even be distinguished.

Now, let's look at the key blockchain technology disadvantages. Despite all the advantages of the blockchain, today this technology cannot be called ideal. It has some drawbacks that programmers from around the world are working to eliminate. We talk about the following things:

- Low translation speed in case of database congestion. Functioning the blockchain requires very large capacities. Therefore, the creation and verification of new blocks can take considerable time. For example, in a Bitcoin system, one transaction can take up to 4-5 hours or more.

- Uncertain regulatory status: It can be said that blockchain and cryptocurrencies are outside the legislative framework of most countries. It is possible to use cryptocurrencies in payments on the network at your own peril and risk, because they are not regulated by law.

- The initial high cost of introducing the technology. Using the blockchain in the transfer of electronic values, you can significantly save on paying for intermediaries and guarantors. However, the very creation of a system and its implementation in any area is very costly.

- As you can see, the technology flaws cannot be called catastrophically serious. It is also important to remember that programmers around the world are working to eliminate them.

Blockchain technology might be used in the stated areas:

- Network Administration

- Digital certificates (storage);

- Bilateral transactions (does not involve any guarantees from a third party in the form of a notary public, a bank, any law firm, and so on);

- Authentication

- Proof of Rights.

In fact, current cryptocurrencies have made it understood by modern users that blockchain technology is a very important element.

Chapter 4 – Transactions in blockchain network

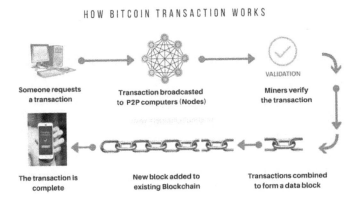

HOW BITCOIN TRANSACTION WORKS

Someone requests a transaction

Transaction broadcasted to P2P computers (Nodes)

Miners verify the transaction

VALIDATION

The transaction is complete

New block added to existing Blockchain

Transactions combined to form a data block

Actually, Bitcoin is the digital currency which appeared the first to be known. If we compare it with the electronic money, here we will see the most impressive difference. Particularly, it does not even exist as a digital file. It is a plenty of information with all transactions ever completed. Most frequently, it possesses the form of a huge accounting book affordable for everybody.

For each transaction, a commission is assigned that is not tied to the transfer amount. It works as a bonus for miners who are involved in job validation.

If the sender receives a lot of transfers with insignificant amounts or often spends the same money, the fee recommended by the wallet for a new payment will be large.

If the sender initially puts a large amount into the wallet and spends a significant amount of coins, the transaction fee will be insignificant. If the sender wants to transfer coins as soon as possible, he can use one of these methods:

- Increase commission for miners;

- Increase the amount of funds transferred;

- Use cryptocurrency exchanges;

- Use bitcoin wallets with the function of creating multi-signature.

The main mistake of most users is that they estimate the size of the commission in absolute terms and do not take into account the size of the transaction itself. Because of this, there are times when a payment freezes on the network for several days.

To fake a transaction, hackers must have significant powers, which in many ways exceed the powers of the sender and receiver. But this is virtually impossible due to 6 confirmations.

In time and under favorable circumstances, confirmation takes about an hour - 1 block = 10 minutes. Users who have more than 10% of capacity (that is, millions of dollars in investment in computing power) receive six confirmations quickly. The sender can reduce the number of checks. The growth of network congestion always causes users to panic, and many do not wait for the set time.

Bitcoins that are issued by the network for finding a block can be used only after 100 confirmations - 100 blocks found. A well-intentioned classic Bitcoin user does not display the coins received for the decision of the block until 120 confirmations are accumulated.

Chapter 5 – Precise overview of the most popular projects done on blockchain technology

According to experts, the volume of the international blockchain industry will reach more than $ 60 billion already in 2024, as more and more companies begin to use distributed registry technology and the use of this technology is becoming widespread. Despite being in the early stages of its growth, the blockchain technology is carefully studied and adjusted by such world famous conglomerates as IBM and Softbank.

As well, a lot of up-to-date enterprises in most countries are solving the problems of market imperfections by effectively using the opportunities provided by blockchain technology. Such companies are found in almost all industries, from dealing with information and transportation services to financial institutions.

The blockchain system is thriving thanks to a well-structured organization, developers, service companies, and businessmen who create a new look for the business market.

PATRON is leading Japanese blockchain company. Currently, its members are creating a decentralized promotion platform with the help of public opinion leaders in order to eliminate the inefficiency of social media marketing. Recently, the company made a profit of $ 40 million from the sale of tokens and is entering the American market.

Founded by public opinion leader Atsushi Hisatsumi, PATRON attracted the attention of the international community through strategic collaboration as well as a strong team of advisers, consisting of industry leaders and blockchain experts.

TraDove has made an easy, fast and reliable blockchain system of payments between legal entities for global business transactions. The enterprise completed the development of great cryptocurrency primary offering systems in 2018. She launched the world's first cryptocurrency settlement system between legal entities, partnership channels from companies to customers, opened up the need for cryptocurrencies for advertisement industry, in fact a new market with a turnover of $ 76 million.

TraDove's corporate network gets sellers familiar with the buyers to have a fast search for offers and high transparency of operations.

Celsius is involved in cryptocurrency banking. Their platform allows getting 5% profit for their cryptocurrency, or take credit at 9%, using cryptocurrency for their benefits. The goal of this financial and technological startup is to replace the traditional banking system.

Menlo One represents a platform for creating decentralized applications that run at the same pace with the regular web applications. Their proven track record algorithm is innovative for decentralized applications. One of the components of a multi-level platform called HashGuilds encourages other more experienced users to create reviews, evaluate and signal high-quality ICOs for all users of the platform.

Managed by TED employee Matthew Nolan it has serious professional qualities, and their primary cryptocurrency placement system deserves attention.

Goldilock's primary goal is to adjust the way we store and secure data on he world wide web. Their innovations allow individual users and entire organizations to safely store digital media in a storage which is not switched to the Internet until the user wants to have connection for their own needs.

The foundation of Goldilock Security is a patented, remotely activated security system enabled by a command that is not transmitted over IP. This allows you to ensure the reliable preservation of cryptocurrency keys and the storage of important digital tools.

Founded by Tzang Jian, the former head of **FCoin**, is a cryptocurrency system with location in China. FCoin is based on mining and profit distribution with the goal to pay 80% back.

Cryptocurrencies are becoming mainstream. Not only do technology startups are introducing technical innovations but also such companies as IBM, Softbank, SAP, BP, Samsung, etc.

Chapter 6 – Cryptocurrencies based on blockchain technologies

Any electronic payment system must somewhere and somehow store transactions. Let's start with the most important cryptocurrency that functions on blockchain technology.

In **Bitcoin**, all information is stored in a chain of blocks. Blocks are transmitted in JSON format. Each block contains a header and a list of transactions. The header consists of several properties, among which is the hash of the previous block. Thus, the entire chain of blocks stores all transactions for the entire duration of Bitcoin.

In current versions of the Bitcoin program, a block chain is downloaded entirely by each client, which makes the system completely decentralized. Data is not encrypted in any way and anyone can manually track all transactions. There is even a special site - Bitcoin Block Explorer, where you can easily see all the information about blocks and transactions.

It works as follows. One of the clients creates a new transaction and sends it to other clients who are busy generating the block. They add this transaction to their block and continue generating. Sooner or later, someone will be able to generate a block. This block is sealed (transactions are no longer added to it) and sent out over the network.

Next, clients check the block and transactions within it for validity. If there are no problems, then transactions are considered approved. At this point, a fresh block has already reached each customer and added to the chain. After this, the process repeats - customers begin to generate the next block and collect new transactions into it.

Proof of work is a result of work that is difficult to achieve but easy to verify. The operation of the Bitcoin network is based on this principle. You can check the hash (the result of work) in a split second. And in order to pick it up, it takes a lot of work.

Here we can recall the analogy with gold, the extraction of which takes a lot of time and resources. But to understand that before you is gold, you can almost immediately. In this sense, Bitcoin also has its value. But do not understand this as the price in dollars or in electricity bills that the computer used during the selection of the hash.

The price in dollars is a little different. It is not inherent in Bitcoin and is determined solely by the market. After all, gold in itself also does not guarantee you a certain price in dollars. It is guaranteed only by a person who wants to exchange gold for dollars.

The initial value of gold was determined solely by those who mined it. For the mined gold, he requested so much that it was possible to compensate for the efforts to mine it. And after that, the market begins to influence the price of gold.

Once Bitcoin entered the market, its value is determined solely by the level of confidence in the system. The more people trust, the more they will buy Bitcoin, the more dollars they will invest in it and, as a result, the more expensive Bitcoin will be.

Before people can trust Bitcoin, they need to find out if this system has a sufficient degree of security, and also whether it can be used as money, i.e., does it have the properties of the money that I listed at the beginning. You can only find out this for sure in the principles of Bitcoin.

Let's go further. The next cryptocurrency is **Ethereum.** It is a public database with the ability to store digital transactions for unlimited time. It is also important to note that no key management systems are required to maintain and protect such a database.

Instead, this platform works as a "defenseless" transaction system - a framework in which individuals can make peer-to-peer transactions, while none of the parties bears any obligations to the other or third parties.

The Ethereum blockchain is essentially a transactional state system. In computer science, such a thing as a "state system" or "state machine" is a system that processes the input information and, based on the latter, is converted into a new state.

In the Ethereum state machine, all processes begin with the "initial state". This state is an analogue of the zero state in which the machine is located until the moment when any actions related to transactions begin to occur in its network. When such actions begin to occur, the initial state is replaced with the final one, and at any moment in time the final state reflects the current state of Ethereum.

Ethereum has millions of transactions. These transactions are grouped into "blocks". A block contains a series of transactions, with each subsequent block connected to the previous one, which ensures a kind of block chain.

A transaction must be correct in order to cause its transition from one state to another. A transaction is considered correct only when it has passed the verification process - the so-called "mining". Mining is when a group of nodes (computers) consumes their computing resources to create a block of correct transactions.

Any node on the network that claims to be a miner can try to create and verify a block of transactions. A common experience is attempts by many miners to simultaneously create and verify a block of transactions.

Each miner provides its own mathematical "proof" when sending a block to the blockchain, and this proof acts as a kind of guarantee: if the proof exists, the transactions in the block are considered correct.The miner must provide its mathematical proof faster than any other competitor does in order for its block to be added to the main blockchain.

The process of checking each block, which consists in providing the miner with his mathematical proof, is called "proof of work". The miner, who justifies the new block, receives a certain reward for doing this work. What kind of reward are we talking about?

The Ethereum blockchain uses a built-in digital token, which is called "ether" (from the English ether - "ether"). Each time a miner substantiates his block of transactions, a new token or new ether is created, and the miner receives a reward for its creation.

One of most popular cryptocurrencies is **Ripple** which matters more than just coins. We explain how this system works and whether it is worth investing in it.

Ripple is a global system for cross-currency and gross payments, created in 2012 by Ripple Labs. The main advantage of the network is that it allows you to conduct mutual transfers anywhere in the world in just a few seconds.

The currency exchange scheme in the system is simple. Suppose a person needs to convert Russian rubles (RUR) to Brazilian real (BRL). First, he translates his rubles into the domestic currency of the Ripple system - XRP ("ripple"). Then, a transfer is made to the wallet with reals belonging to the bank. At the end of the operation, the person receives Brazilian currency.

Thanks to xRapid technology, such an exchange takes place in just few seconds. This is one of the main advantages of XRP. In addition, all transfers in the system are revocable, that is, they can be canceled and returned.

The high speed of transfers in Ripple is due to the fact that the network is supported by 14 servers around the world, in contrast to the same bitcoin, which depends on miners, which help to overcome a heavy load. Therefore, this system is so attractive to banks.

Nowadays, more and more banks are switching to Ripple. This excitement allowed XRP to make a huge jump in value. Now this currency by capitalization is in third place ($ 20.2 billion) after Bitcoin ($ 119.9 billion) and Ethereum ($ 39.06 billion).The cost of XRP is $ 0.517754 despite the fact that the rate of this currency depends not only on holders, but also on ordinary transfers.

After all, as described above, XRP is involved in each exchange, and its liquidity is thereby increased. But, contrary to the expectations of many people, in the near future banks are not going to completely switch to XRP, using this currency not only for exchange, but also for transfers.

This is due to the fact that corporations need stability, to which any cryptocurrency is still very far away. Naturally, no one will take the risk of a price collapse at any time, so companies will be wary of XRP for a long time to come. In addition, Ripple Labs recently began to sue R3 for outstanding obligations set forth in the contract. This position of the company is not attractive to large corporations and investors. Moreover, Ripple owns 61 billion of them, and about 300 million XRP is spent on expenses per month.

In addition, 55 billion tokens of those owned by developers are blocked by 55 smart contracts. This policy allows the company to make transfers as transparent as possible. In addition, Ripple Labs thus reduces its chances of bankruptcy, even with a hypothetical ban and the collapse of XRP.

Despite all the advantages of the Ripple network and its internal currency XRP, you cannot trust a centralized system in the cryptocurrency market. When all coins and tokens want to achieve complete independence from the outside world in order to move the economy forward, developers from Ripple Labs increase the number of factors affecting the XRP rate.

Banks and creators have too much share in this currency, so we can safely say that XRP is a corporate centralized currency. Therefore, it cannot be called a full-fledged cryptocurrency, because it does not meet one of the main requirements of the market.

Conclusion

Blockchain is a distributed registry, a database whose users interact directly with each other. The system does not have an intermediary link in the form of a single administrator or a dedicated server that stores information about all operations. Transaction data is available to any member of the network. Users store copies of the registry on their computers.

Transaction data includes:

- the amount of transferred accounting units (cryptocurrencies or tokens),

- signature of the sender

- address of the recipient.

A new operation takes effect only after several independent participants confirm it. After the update, all copies of the registry are automatically synchronized.

Technically, a blockchain is a chain of blocks with data about operations. Each block has a header that contains information about all operations in the block plus data on the contents of the previous block. This sequence is maintained until the very beginning of the chain.

New blocks form miners. These network participants solve the problem - they calculate the only true value (hash) of the block by brute force. The value that the miner should find is set by the system. The miner, who solved the problem first, forms a block and receives a reward. In order to unauthorizedly make changes to the registry, the attacker will have to do the same amount of calculations that the miners needed to form the entire chain of blocks.

Here are the forecasts for the three case study industries listed by CB Insights.

- The blockchain will become the basis for counting votes. The distributed register will record the election results once, and will not allow them to be changed or deleted unnoticed by other participants.

A similar blockchain solution is offered, for example, by Agora Technologies.

- Another case in which the blockchain is used is an accounting registry for authenticating academic data. The technology will serve as a tool to confirm the degree or certificate of completion of the curriculum. In 2017, Sony and IBM joined forces to create such a system.

- In the future, real estate transactions will automatically be recorded on the blockchain. The transfer of property rights will occur not only with the participation of a notary and the registration chamber. The blockchain will act as an independent core for accounting data on transactions and their participants. A similar service was introduced by Ubitquity.

The global scenario for the development of blockchain depends on the final answer to the question: "Is the peak of blockchain hype over or still to come?" The largest research and consulting companies Gartner and McKinsey disagree.

In August 2018, Gartner published a technology maturity curve according to which the blockchain passed the peak of hype and headed towards the "chasm of disappointment." If you stick to this scenario, then the development of corporate blockchain developments and a focus on industry products are quite natural.

In January 2019, McKinsey came to the opposite point of view. According to the report, blockchain is still at an early stage of development and is still far from mass distribution. According to McKinsey representatives, the blockchain has not yet reached the peak of hype, expressed in the growing demand for technology around the world.

If this scenario is true, then the cases listed in the material are either unpromising beginnings or steps towards mass application of the blockchain.